Science to the Rescue
Alone in the Arctic

Can science save your life?

Gerry Bailey

Crabtree Publishing Company
www.crabtreebooks.com

Crabtree Publishing Company
www.crabtreebooks.com
1-800-387-7650

PMB 59051, 350 Fifth Ave.   616 Welland Ave.
59th Floor,   St. Catharines, ON
New York, NY 10118   L2M 5V6

Published by Crabtree Publishing in 2014

Author: Gerry Bailey
Illustrator: Leighton Noyes
Editor: Shirley Duke
Proofreader: Kathy Middleton
**Production coordinator and
    Prepress technician:** Tammy McGarr
Print coordinator: Margaret Amy Salter

Photographs:
All images are Shutterstock.com unless otherwise stated.
Cover - PSD Photography Pg 1 – FotoYakov
Pg 2/3 – FotoYakov Pg 6 – AridOcean
Pg 6/7 – Incredible Arctic Pg 8/9 – ECOSTOCK
Pg 8 – AleksandrN AleksandrN
Pg 9 – (l) Daniel Hebert (m) ericlefrancais
(r) Sergey Uryadnikov Pg 11 – FotoYakov
(t) Barry Blackburn (b) Andrey Shtanko
Pg 12 – Dimos Pg 12/13 - Tyler Olsen
Pg 14/15 – NightOwl Pg 15 – Sergey Nivens
Pg 16 – FotoYakov (m) Andresr
Pg 17 – (t) hainaultphoto (b) Marteric
Pg 19 – Ernest Manewal / SuperStock
Pg 20/21 – Tyler Olsen Pg 21 – Galen Rowell/
Corbis Pg 22 – Nick Cobbing/Alamy Pg 23 – NASA /
Wikipedia.org Pg 26/27 – Jan Martin Will
Pg 29 – Bob Krist/Corbis Pg 30 – FotoYakov
(inset) outdoorsman Pg 32 – (t) Andrey
Siradchuk (m) BigRoloImages (b) Tyler Olsen
Icicles frieze - Roman Malyshev

Printed in Canada/032014/BF20140212

Library and Archives Canada Cataloguing in Publication

Bailey, Gerry, author
    Alone in the Arctic / Gerry Bailey.

(Science to the rescue)
Includes index.
Issued in print and electronic formats.
ISBN 978-0-7787-0428-7 (bound).--ISBN 978-0-7787-0434-8 (pbk.).--
ISBN 978-1-4271-7540-3 (html).--ISBN 978-1-4271-7546-5 (pdf)

    1. Arctic regions--Juvenile literature. I. Title.

G614.B35 2014   j919.8   C2014-900920-8
                                       C2014-900921-6

Library of Congress Cataloging-in-Publication Data

CIP available at Library of Congress

Contents

Joe's story

Hi! My name is Joe, and I have
a story to tell you—
a real adventure!

I got stranded on the ice.
I thought I wouldn't make it
back to the safety of the
base—but I did! Just barely!

I managed to survive with
the help of all the science
I know. But it's a long story.

This story gets really chilly!
Everyone huddle up,
and I'll begin.

My story is set here in the Arctic. I imagine you know where that is—the most northern part of the globe surrounding the North Pole.

It's very cold up here. Ice and snow stretches into the distance as far as the eye can see—ice and snow, and not much else.

North Pole

United States

Norway

Finland

Russia

Greenland

Canada

South Pole

Where is the Arctic?

The Arctic is the region around the North Pole. There is no land there, only sea and ice. In fact, the Arctic is a large frozen ocean, or **ice sheet**, that never completely melts.

The largest **ice shelf** in the Arctic is **Ward Hunt Ice Shelf**. This single piece of ice is the size of 11,000 soccer fields. However, this ice shelf is beginning to melt and break apart because Earth is warming up.

The Arctic ice sheet is bordered by six countries. They are Canada, Russia, Finland, Norway, Greenland, and the United States.

During the short summers, the ice sheet shrinks. In winter when the temperature drops, it grows again.

Well, maybe you'll see a walrus or two. Big, gray, blubbery walruses with two long tusks. Oh, and seals—there are a few seals...and silvery white foxes...and owls...and polar bears.

Okay, so maybe it isn't JUST ice and snow!

Thick layers of fat, called blubber, keep a walrus warm in icy waters.

Harp seals are gray, but the babies are white making them hard to see.

What animals live there?

The arctic, or snowy, owl has lots of thick feathers on its feet.

The fur of the arctic fox is brown in summer and white in winter.

Polar bears dig homes, called dens, in the snow.

You're getting impatient. You want to hear the story.

My fellow scientists and I were in the Arctic to study changes in the ice. We were heading back to our base at the weather station. On the way, a **blizzard** blew up. You don't want to be out on the ice in a blizzard.

Howling gales...freezing your clothing.

Blinding snow... freezing your hair.

Icy winds... freezing your breath!

Brrr! It was cold like you've never felt in your life.

Exactly how cold?

The Arctic climate has cold winters and cool summers. There's not much rainfall. When there is, it falls as snow. High winds often stir up snow, and this makes it seem as if snow is falling all the time. In winter, the temperature can be as low as -40° Fahrenheit (-40° Celsius). The coldest it has ever been was -90°F (-68°C).

You know how cold the food in your refrigerator's freezer gets? That's only about 0°F (-18°C), so the Arctic is a lot colder!

The freezing point of water is 32°F (0°C).

Ice cream stays frozen in your freezer at 23°F (-5°C). If the temperature increases, it will start to melt.

11

Racing across the ice on our **snowmobiles**, we were moving in a long line. I was at the back—quite a long way back.

And suddenly—CRICK! CRACK! The ice broke in front of me.

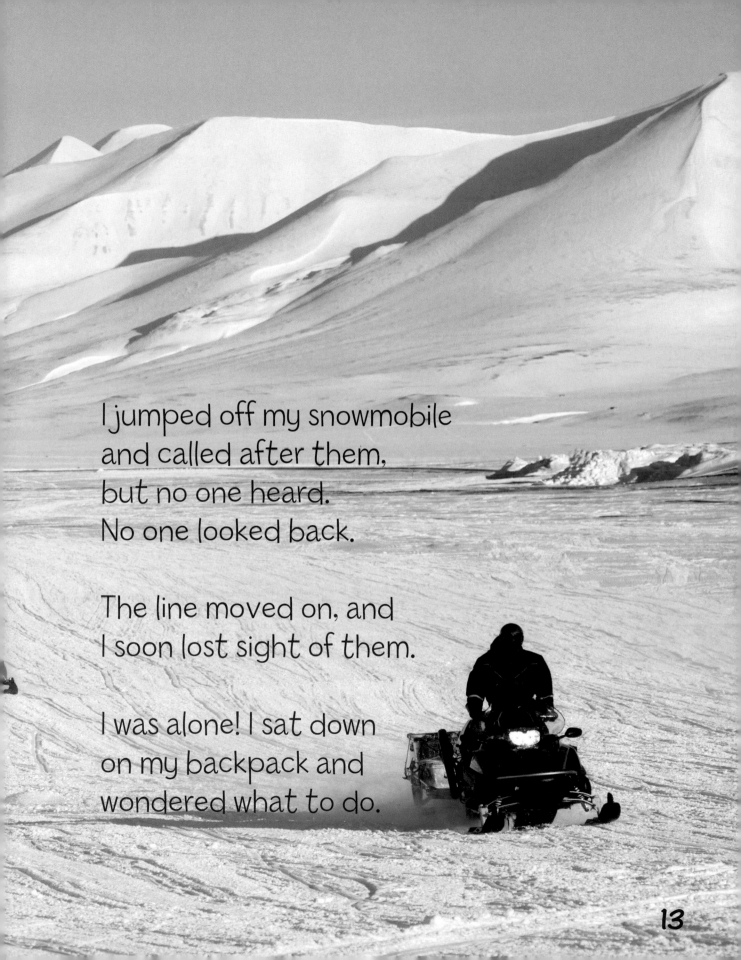

I jumped off my snowmobile
and called after them,
but no one heard.
No one looked back.

The line moved on, and
I soon lost sight of them.

I was alone! I sat down
on my backpack and
wondered what to do.

I was stuck on a piece of ice that had broken free and was drifting into the ocean.

I sat on the edge of the ice and tried to convince myself how great it was to be living on an **iceberg**! But it wasn't. I knew I had to build myself a shelter.

But, what with? Then I remembered the native **Inuit** build shelters out of ice. Why couldn't I?

What is an iceberg?

An iceberg is a large piece of ice made of fresh water that has broken off from a **glacier** or ice shelf. To be classified as an iceberg, ice must be 50 feet (15 m) long and 16 feet (5 m) above the water, or it is just a piece of floating ice.

Only about one-ninth of an iceberg can be seen above water.

How do you build an igloo?

The snow used to build an **igloo** must have enough strength to be cut and stacked in a spiral pattern.

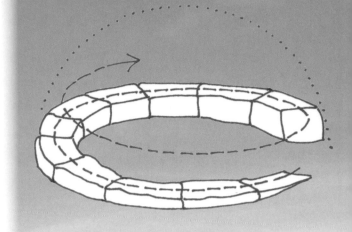

An igloo needs to be built in a **dome** shape. A dome uses ice blocks that lock together to make a very light but very strong structure.

Separate blocks are stacked on top of each other and rubbed into shape at the end.

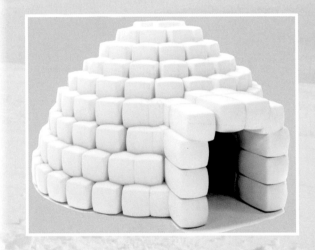

Sometimes, a short tunnel is constructed at the entrance to reduce heat loss when the door is opened.

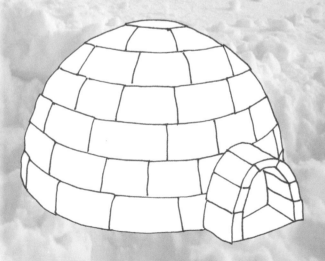

Snow blown by the wind makes the best building material. It is more packed and the ice crystals are connected tightly together. Pockets of air inside the snow provide good insulation, keeping the heat in.

The roofs of mosques and many other religious or government buildings around the world are dome-shaped.

The heat from a lamp inside the igloo also makes the inside wall of blocks melt slightly. This melting and freezing packs the ice blocks together.

The finished igloo

Outside, it may be -49°F (-45°C), but on the inside, your body heat alone keeps it closer to 19°F (-7°C).

An igloo that is built correctly will support the weight of a person standing on the roof.

I was pretty pleased with my igloo, but all the hard work had made me hungry. Where would I find food?

I remembered a trick that is used by the local people. They cut a hole in the ice, put bait on a fishing line, and dangle the bait in the sea. When a fish bites, they spear it and pull it out of the hole.

I found what I needed in my backpack, and at last I caught a fish. I cut it into thin strips. It tasted good!

18

Fish of the Arctic

cod (up to 15.7 in/40cm)

skate (up to 3.3 ft/1 m)

shark (up to 10 ft/3.1 m)

flatfish
(up to 20.5 in/52 cm)

lumpsucker
(up to 19.7 in/50 cm)

An Inuit woman is jigging for fish through a hole in the ice.

How do you catch fish?

Inuits catch fish using a skill they call jigging. The hunter cuts a hole in the ice and fishes using a fake fish attached to a line as bait. They lower this into the water and move it around as if it were real. When the live fish approaches, they spear the fish before it has a chance to eat the bait.

Who lives in the Arctic?

Many people live in the Arctic despite the cold! Of course, life is hard and people have learned to be hardy to survive.

The Inuit people live in Canada and Greenland. They protect themselves from the bitter cold with clothing made from reindeer and seal skins and the furs of wolves and polar bears. To move from place to place, the Inuit use snow machines called snowmobiles. They wear skis and wide-soled snowshoes so their feet won't sink into the soft snow.

The Lapp people live in northern Scandinavia. They used to move from place to place with their herds of reindeer. Today most Lapps do not follow the traditional nomadic life and live in cities instead.

A snowmobile moves over the ice.

An Inuit family

The **Chukchi** people of Arctic Russia used to hunt walruses and whales in canoes called kayaks. The boats were made of skins stretched over a frame. Today they use motorboats and snowmobiles.

I was beginning to feel quite lonely. I needed someone to talk to.

AND I was beginning to get worried about my floating home. It was definitely getting smaller. The ice that made up my small iceberg was melting, much like it was melting on the WHOLE Arctic **ice cap**.

Scientists have been studying the effects of **global warming**—the gradual rise in Earth's temperature—for many years. When people burn coal, gas, and oil, it releases more and more carbon dioxide into the atmosphere. This buildup of gas holds more heat in and warms Earth.

A scientist measures a sample of ice to record its length.

The Arctic has suffered more than any other part of the planet from global warming. The polar ice that makes up the whole region is melting so fast that it may all be gone in as little as twenty years.

What happens if the ice cap melts?

As the ice sheets melt and release water into the seas, the level of the oceans rise. Over time, this will cause flooding in many parts of the world close to sea level. Soil will be washed away, and homes and crops will be damaged.

The Arctic ice cap was this big in 1984.

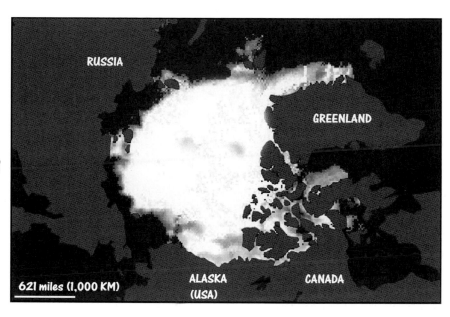

621 miles (1,000 KM)

The oceans influence weather on Earth. The temperature of ocean waters plays a big part in creating storms and hurricanes, which cause flooding and destruction.

By 2012, a huge region of the ice cap had melted.

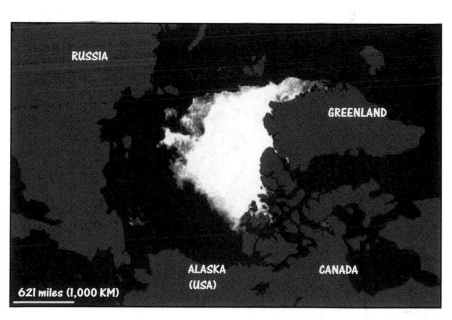

621 miles (1,000 KM)

But that night,
I heard a slobbery,
slubbery sound.
The ice rocked.

Something slobbered
and slubbered
past my igloo...
and I didn't dare look!

The next morning, there it was.

A big, brown, blubbery walrus
with two long tusks was sitting
on my piece of ice with its
whiskers twitching.

I looked at the walrus,
and the walrus looked back.

Then it yawned, lay down on its
stomach, and slept.

24

"Good!" I said. "Now I have some wildlife to enjoy."

All that day, the wildlife just kept coming to me.

A family of seals,

two snow geese,

a snowy owl,

and a polar bear...

We were quite a strange family...

more like a floating zoo!

And when the boat
finally found me,
I was actually sad.

I waved good-bye to them all,
and I like to think they were
waving back as they floated
away across the ocean.

Why is Joe there?

Joe is a scientist. He is part of a team that has been monitoring the temperatures and ice loss in the Arctic over many years. Scientists like Joe, from countries all over the world, have set up special bases where they live and work at certain times of the year.

At the base, they collect data from weather-tracking satellites and they watch the movement of the ice. They note how the glaciers move out to sea and the speed they travel. They know that melting ice from the ice sheets will result in rising ocean levels.

Huge ships called **icebreakers**, like the Amundsen shown here, check on the ice each year in the northern seas of Canada. The ship comes to a halt when it finds the ice too thick. On its most recent trip, however, it was able to keep going for the first time. This shows how thin the ice has become.

Glossary

base
The home location and starting point for an expedition

blizzard
A severe snowstorm with very high winds. It usually lasts for several hours and reduces visibility.

Chukchi
An East Russian people who live on the Chukchi peninsula and along the shores of the Chukchi and Bering seas.

dome
A strong structure used in building that is in the shape of a hollow half-sphere.

glacier
Snow compacted into a valley and built up. Snow turns to ice from the weight and this causes the river of ice to flow slowly downhill.

global warming
The gradual increase of the temperature in Earth's atmosphere from heat-trapping gases released by the burning of fossil fuels

iceberg
Chunks of a glacier or ice shelf after it breaks off and falls into the sea

icebreakers
Ships with a specially designed hull, or body, that can push through ice

ice cap
A sheet of ice caused by glaciers building up over continental areas and moving outwards. The main ice caps are the Antarctic and Greenland ice caps.

ice sheet
A layer of frozen water that shrinks in summer but expands again in winter

ice shelf
A platform of ice that forms where a glacier or ice sheet on land flows from the shore out into the sea

igloo
A round house built from blocks of ice by Inuit people

Inuit
Indigenous, or native, people who live in the Arctic region of Canada

snowmobile
Small vehicles with runners at the front and a revolving tread at the rear that travel over snow and ice

Ward Hunt Ice Shelf
Located on Canada's north coast, the Ward Hunt is the largest ice sheet in the Arctic. It's almost 250 square miles (400 sq km) in size.

Learn More...

Books:

Keep On!: The Story of Matthew Henson, Co-Discoverer of the North Pole
by Deborah Hopkinson.
Peachtree Publishers, 2009

Amazing Arctic & Antarctic Projects You Can Build Yourself
By Carmella Van Vleet.
Nomad Press, 2008

Geodesic Domes
by Borin Van Loon.
Parkwest Publications, 1994

Websites:

Learn all about dome structures around the world.
http://architecture.about.com/od/domes/tp/Great-Domes.htm

An interesting list of Arctic explorers and their expeditions. http://
www.enchantedlearning.com/explorers/arctic.shtml

Learn all about ice shelves and climate change.
http://nsidc.org/cryosphere/sotc/iceshelves.html

Index